The Wit
and
Wisdom
of
Abraham
Lincoln

FLEMING H. REVELL COMPANY
OLD TAPPAN • NEW JERSEY

CONTENTS

I   SPEECHES   5

II   AUTOBIOGRAPHICAL   17

III   LETTERS TO HIS STEPBROTHER   29

IV   LETTERS TO LADIES   37

V   LETTERS TO GENERALS   47

VI   WIT AND WISDOM   55

I

Speeches

FROM A SPEECH POKING FUN AT PRESIDENTIAL CANDIDATE LEWIS CASS
July 27, 1848

... in my hurry I was very near closing on the subject of military tails before I was done with it. There is one entire article of the sort I have not discussed yet; I mean the military tail you Democrats are now engaged in dovetailing on to the great Michigander. Yes sir, all his biographers (and they are legion) have him in hand, tying him to a military tail, like so many mischievous boys tying a dog to a bladder of beans. True, the material they have is very limited; but they drive at it, might and main. He *in*vaded Canada without resistance, and he *out*vaded it without pursuit. As he did both under orders, I suppose there was, to him, neither credit or discredit in them; but they are made to constitute a large part of the tail. He was not at Hull's surrender, but he was close by; he was volunteer aid to Gen. Harrison on the day of the Battle of the Thames; and, as you said in 1840, Harrison was picking huckleberries two miles off while the battle was fought, I suppose it is a just conclusion with you to say Cass was aiding Harrison to pick huckleberries. This is about all, except the mooted question of the broken sword. Some authors say he broke it, some say he threw it away, and some others who ought to know, say nothing about it. Perhaps it would be a fair historical compromise to say, if he did not break it he didn't do anything else with it.

By the way, Mr. Speaker, did you know I am a military hero? Yes sir; in the days of the Black Hawk war, I fought, bled, and came away. Speaking of Gen. Cass's career reminds me of my own. I was not at Stillman's defeat, but I was about as near it as Cass was to Hull's surrender; and, like him, I saw the place very soon afterwards. It is quite

7

certain I did not break my sword, for I had none to break; but I bent a musket pretty badly on one occasion. If Cass broke his sword, the idea is, he broke it in desperation; I bent the musket by accident. If Gen. Cass went in advance of me in picking huckleberries, I guess I surpassed him in charges upon the wild onions. If he saw any live, fighting Indians, it was more than I did; but I had a good many bloody struggles with the mosquitoes; and, although I never fainted from loss of blood, I can truly say I was often very hungry. Mr. Speaker, if I should ever conclude to doff whatever our Democratic friends may suppose there is of black cockade Federalism about me, and thereupon they shall take me up as their candidate for the Presidency, I protest they shall not make fun of me, as they have of Gen. Cass, by attempting to write me into a military hero.

FAREWELL ADDRESS AT SPRINGFIELD, ILLINOIS
February 11, 1861

My Friends:

No one, not in my situation, can appreciate my feeling of sadness at this parting. To this place, and the kindness of these people, I owe everything. Here I have lived a quarter of a century, and have passed from a young to an old man. Here my children have been born, and one is buried. I now leave, not knowing when or whether ever I may return, with a task before me greater than that which rested upon Washington. Without the assistance of that Divine Being who ever attended him, I cannot succeed. With that assistance, I cannot fail. Trusting in Him who can go with me, and remain with you, and be everywhere for good, let us confidently hope that all will yet be well.

To His care commending you, as I hope in your prayers you will commend me, I bid you an affectionate farewell.

FROM THE FIRST INAUGURAL ADDRESS
March 4, 1861

Why should there not be a patient confidence in the ultimate justice of the people? Is there any better or equal hope, in the world? In our present differences, is either party without faith of being in the right? If the Almighty Ruler of nations, with his eternal truth and justice, be on your side of the North or on yours of the South, that truth, and that justice, will surely prevail, by the judgment of this great tribunal, the American people.

By the frame of the government under which we live, this same people have wisely given their public servants but little power for mischief; and have, with equal wisdom, provided for the return of that little to their own hands at very short intervals.

While the people retain their virtue and vigilance, no administration, by any extreme of wickedness or folly, can very seriously injure the government in the short space of four years.

My countrymen, one and all, think calmly and *well,* upon this whole subject. Nothing valuable can be lost by taking time. If there be an object to *hurry* any of you, in hot haste, to a step which you would never take *deliberately,* that object will be frustrated by taking time; but no good object can be frustrated by it. Such of you as are now dissatisfied, still have the old Constitution unimpaired, and, on the sensitive point, the laws of your own framing under it; while the new administration will have no immediate power, if it would, to change either. If it were admitted that you who are dissatisfied, hold the right side in the dispute, there still is no single good reason for precipitate action. Intelligence, patriotism, Christianity, and a firm reliance on Him, who has never yet forsaken this favored land, are still competent to adjust, in the best way, all our present difficulty.

In *your* hands, my dissatisfied fellow countrymen, and not in *mine,* is the momentous issue of civil war. The government will not assail *you.* You can have no conflict, without being yourselves the aggressors. *You* have no oath registered in Heaven to destroy the government, while *I* shall have the most solemn one to "preserve, protect and defend" it.

I am loth to close. We are not enemies, but friends. We must not be enemies. Though passion may have strained, it must not break our bonds of affection. The mystic chords of memory, stretching from every battle-field, and patriot grave, to every living heart and hearth-stone, all over this broad land, will yet swell the chorus of the Union, when again touched, as surely they will be, by the better angels of our nature.

FROM THE ANNUAL MESSAGE TO CONGRESS
December 1, 1862

Fellow-citizens, we cannot escape history. We of this Congress and this administration will be remembered in spite of ourselves. No personal significance or insignificance can spare one or another of us. The fiery trial through which we pass will light us down, in honor or dishonor, to the latest generation. We say we are for the Union. The world will not forget that we say this. We know how to save the Union. The world knows we do know how to save it. We—even we here—hold the power and bear the responsibility. In giving freedom to the slave, we assure freedom to the free—honorable alike in what we give and what we preserve. We shall nobly save or meanly lose the last, best hope of earth. Other means may succeed; this could not fail. The way is plain, peaceful, generous, just —a way which, if followed, the world will forever applaud, and God must forever bless.

THE GETTYSBURG ADDRESS
November 19, 1863

Four score and seven years ago our fathers brought forth on this continent, a new nation, conceived in Liberty, and dedicated to the proposition that all men are created equal.

Now we are engaged in a great civil war, testing whether that nation, or any nation so conceived and so dedicated, can long endure. We are met on a great battle-field of that war. We have come to dedicate a portion of that field, as a final resting place for those who here gave their lives that that nation might live. It is altogether fitting and proper that we should do this.

But, in a larger sense, we can not dedicate—we can not consecrate—we can not hallow—this ground. The brave men, living and dead, who struggled here, have consecrated it, far above our poor power to add or detract. The world will little note, nor long remember what we say here, but it can never forget what they did here. It is for us the living, rather, to be dedicated here to the unfinished work which they who fought here have thus far so nobly advanced. It is rather for us to be here dedicated to the great task remaining before us—that from these honored dead we take increased devotion to that cause for which they gave the last full measure of devotion—that we here highly resolve that these dead shall not have died in vain—that this nation, under God, shall have a new birth of freedom—and that government of the people, by the people, for the people, shall not perish from the earth.

Abraham Lincoln.

FROM A SPEECH IN BALTIMORE
April 18, 1864

The world has never had a good definition of the word liberty, and the American people, just now, are much in want of one. We all declare for liberty; but in using the same *word* we do not all mean the same *thing*. With some the word liberty may mean for each man to do as he pleases with himself, and the product of his labour; while with others the same word may mean for some men to do as they please with other men, and the product of other men's labour. Here are two, not only different, but incompatible things, called by the same name—liberty. And it follows that each of the things is, by the respective parties, called by two different and incompatible names—liberty and tyranny.

SPEECH TO THE 166TH OHIO REGIMENT
August 22, 1864

I suppose you are going home to see your families and friends. For the service you have done in this great struggle in which we are engaged I present you sincere thanks for myself and the country. I almost always feel inclined, when I happen to say anything to soldiers, to impress upon them in a few brief remarks the importance of success in this contest. It is not merely for today, but for all time to come that we should perpetuate for our children's children this great and free government, which we have enjoyed all our lives. I beg you to remember this, not merely for my sake, but for yours. I happen temporarily to occupy this big White House. I am a living witness that any one of your children may look to come here as my father's child has. It is in order that each of you may have through this free government which we have enjoyed, an open field and a fair chance for your industry, enterprise and intelligence; that you may all have equal privileges in the race of life, with all its desirable human aspirations. It is for this the struggle should be maintained, that we may not lose our birthright—not only for one, but for two or three years. The nation is worth fighting for, to secure such an inestimable jewel.

SECOND INAUGURAL ADDRESS
March 4, 1865

At this second appearing to take the oath of the presidential office, there is less occasion for an extended address than there was at the first. Then a statement, somewhat in detail, of a course to be pursued, seemed fitting and proper. Now, at the expiration of four years, during which public declarations have been constantly called forth on every point and phase of the great contest which still absorbs the attention, and engrosses the energies of the nation, little that is new could be presented. The progress of our arms, upon which all else chiefly depends, is as well known to the public as to myself; and it is, I trust, reasonably satisfactory and encouraging to all. With high hope for the future, no prediction in regard to it is ventured.

On the occasion corresponding to this four years ago, all thoughts were anxiously directed to an impending civil war. All dreaded it—all sought to avert it. While the inaugeral [sic] address was being delivered from this place, devoted altogether to *saving* the Union without war, insurgent agents were in the city seeking to *destroy* it without war—seeking to dissole [*sic*] the Union, and divide effects, by negotiation. Both parties deprecated war; but one of them would *make* war rather than let the nation survive; and the other would *accept* war rather than let it perish. And the war came.

One eighth of the whole population were colored slaves, not distributed generally over the Union, but localized in the Southern part of it. These slaves constituted a peculiar and powerful interest. All knew that this interest was, somehow, the cause of the war. To strengthen, perpetuate, and extend this interest was the object for which the insurgents would rend the Union, even by war; while the government claimed no right to do more than to restrict the territorial enlargement of it. Neither party expected for the war, the magnitude, or the duration, which it has already attained. Neither anticipated that the *cause* of the conflict might cease with, or even before, the conflict itself should cease. Each looked for an easier triumph, and a result less fundamental and astounding. Both read the same Bible, and pray to the same God; and each invokes His aid against the other. It may seem strange that any men should dare to ask a just God's assistance in wringing their bread from the sweat of other men's faces; but let us judge not that we be not judged. The prayers of both could not be answered; that of neither has been answered fully. The Almighty has his own purposes. "Woe unto the world because of offences! for it must needs be that offences come; but woe to that man by whom the offence cometh!" If we shall suppose that American Slavery is one of those offences which, in the providence of God, must needs come, but which, having continued through His appointed time, He now wills to remove, and

14

that He gives to both North and South, this terrible war, as the woe due to those by whom the offence came, shall we discern therein any departure from those divine attributes which the believers in a Living God always ascribe to Him? Fondly do we hope—fervently do we pray—that this mighty scourge of war may speedily pass away. Yet, if God wills that it continue, until all the wealth piled by the bond-man's two hundred and fifty years of unrequited toil shall be sunk, and until every drop of blood drawn with the lash, shall be paid by another drawn with the sword, as was said three thousand years ago, so still it must be said "the judgments of the Lord, are true and righteous altogether"

With malice toward none; with charity for all; with firmness in the right, as God gives us to see the right, let us strive on to finish the work we are in; to bind up the nation's wounds; to care for him who shall have borne the battle, and for his widow, and his orphan—to do all which may achieve and cherish a just and lasting peace, among ourselves, and with all nations.

AT A SERENADE THE DAY AFTER THE NORTHERN VICTORY
April 10, 1865

I have always thought 'Dixie' one of the best tunes I have ever heard. Our adversaries over the way attempted to appropriate it, but I insisted yesterday that we fairly captured it. I presented the question to the Attorney General, and he gave it as his legal opinion that it is our lawful prize. I now request the band to favour me with its performance.

II

Autobiographical

AUTOBIOGRAPHY

I was born Feb. 12, 1809, in Hardin County, Kentucky. My parents were both born in Virginia, of undistinguished families—second families, perhaps I should say. My mother, who had died in my tenth year, was of a family of the name of Hanks, some of whom now reside in Adams, and others in Macon Counties, Illinois. My paternal grandfather, Abraham Lincoln, emigrated from Rockingham County, Virginia, to Kentucky, about 1781 or 2, where, a year or two later, he was killed by indians, not in battle, but by stealth, when he was laboring to open a farm in the forest. His ancestors, who were Quakers, went to Virginia from Berks County, Pennsylvania. An effort to identify them with the New-England family of the same name ended in nothing more definite, than a similarity of Christian names in both families, such as Enoch, Levi, Mordecai, Solomon, Abraham, and the like.

My father, at the death of his father, was but six years of age; and he grew up, litterally [*sic*] without education. He removed from Kentucky to what is now Spencer County, Indiana, in my eighth year. We reached our new home about the time the State came into the Union. It was a wild region, with many bears and other wild animals, still in the woods. There I grew up. There were some schools, so called; but no qualification was ever required of a teacher beyond "readin, writin, and cipherin" to the Rule of Three. If a straggler supposed to understand latin happened to sojourn in the neighborhood, he was looked upon as a wizzard [*sic*]. There was absolutely nothing to excite ambition for education. Of course when

19

I came of age I did not know much. Still somehow, I could read, write, and cipher to the Rule of Three; but that was all. I have not been to school since. The little advance I now have upon this store of education, I have picked up from time to time under the pressure of necessity.

I was raised to farm work, which I continued till I was twenty-two. At twenty one I came to Illinois, and passed the first year in Macon County. Then I got to New-Salem (at that time in Sangamon, now in Menard County), where I remained a year as a sort of Clerk in a store. Then came the Black-Hawk war; and I was elected a Captain of Volunteers—a success which gave me more pleasure than any I have had since. I went the campaign, was elated, ran for the Legislature the same year (1832) and was beaten—the only time I ever have been beaten by the people. The next, and three succeeding biennial elections, I was elected to the Legislature. I was not a candidate afterwards. During this Legislative period I had studied law, and removed to Springfield to practise it. In 1846 I was once elected to the lower House of Congress. Was not a candidate for re-election. From 1849 to 1854, both inclusive, practiced law more assiduously than ever before. Always a whig in politics, and generally on the whig electoral tickets, making active canvasses—I was losing interest in politics, when the repeal of the Missouri Compromise aroused me again. What I have done since then is pretty well known.

If any personal description of me is thought desirable, it may be said, I am, in height, six feet, four inches, nearly; lean in flesh, weighing on an average one hundred and eighty pounds; dark complexion, with coarse black hair, and grey eyes—no other marks or brands recollected.

FROM AN ADDRESS TO THE
NEW JERSEY SENATE, TRENTON
February 21, 1861

. . . away back in my childhood, the earliest days of
my being able to read, I got hold of a small book, such
a one as few of the younger members have ever seen,
Weems's *Life of Washington*. I remember all the accounts
there given of the battle-fields and struggles for the liberties
of the country, and none fixed themselves upon my imagi-
nation so deeply as the struggle here at Trenton, New Jersey. The crossing of the river, the contest with the Hessians,
the great hardships endured at that time, all fixed themselves on my memory more than any single revolutionary
event; and you all know, for you have all been boys, how
these early impressions last longer than any others. I recol-
lect thinking then, boy even though I was, that there must
have been something more than common that those men
struggled for.

FROM A LETTER
February 25, 1842

My old Father used to have a saying that "If you make
a bad bargain, *hug* it all the tighter". . . .

ANNOUNCEMENT OF POLITICAL VIEWS

New Salem, June 13, 1836.

To the Editor of the Journal:

In your paper of last Saturday, I see a communication,
over the signature of "Many Voters," in which the candi-
dates who are announced in the Journal, are called upon to
"show their hands." Agreed. Here's mine!

I go for all sharing the privileges of the government, who assist in bearing its burthens. Consequently I go for admitting all whites to the right of suffrage, who pay taxes or bear arms, (by no means excluding females.)

If elected, I shall consider the whole people of Sangamon my constituents, as well those that oppose, as those that support me.

While acting as their representative, I shall be governed by their will, on all subjects upon which I have the means of knowing what their will is; and upon all others, I shall do what my own judgment teaches me will best advance their interests. Whether elected or not, I go for distributing the proceeds of the sales of the public lands to the several states, to enable our state, in common with others, to dig canals and construct rail roads, without borrowing money and paying interest on it.

If alive on the first Monday in November, I shall vote for Hugh L. White for President.

Very respectfully,
A. Lincoln

LETTER TO WILLIAM G. ANDERSON, A POLITICAL OPPONENT

Lawrenceville, Illinois, 31st October, 1840.

Dear Sir: Your note of yesterday is received. In the difficulty between us, of which you speak, you say you think I was the aggressor. I do not think I was. You say my "words imported insult." I meant them as a fair set-off to your own statements, and not otherwise; and in that light alone I now wish you to understand them. You ask for my "present feelings on the subject." I entertain no unkind feeling to you, and none of any sort upon the subject, except a sincere regret that I permitted myself to get into such an altercation. Yours, etc.

A. Lincoln

FROM A LETTER TO JOHN T. STUART

Springfield, 23rd January 1841.

. . . For not giving you a general summary of news, you *must* pardon me; it is not in my power to do so. I am now the most miserable man living. If what I feel were equally distributed to the whole human family, there would not be one cheerful face on the earth. Whether I shall ever be better I cannot tell; I awfully forebode I shall not. To remain as I am is impossible; I must die or be better, it appears to me. The matter you speak of on my account, you may attend to as you say, unless you shall hear of my condition forbidding it. I say this because I fear I shall be unable to attend to any business here, and a change of scene might help me. If I could be myself I would rather remain at home with Judge Logan. I can write no more. Your friend, as ever

A. Lincoln

FROM A LETTER
November 11, 1842

. . . Nothing new here, except my marrying, which to me, is matter of profound wonder.

TO RICHARD S. THOMAS, A WHIG RESIDING IN LINCOLN'S CONGRESSIONAL DISTRICT

Springfield, 14th February 1843.

Friend Richard: . . . Now if you should hear anyone say that Lincoln don't want to go to Congress, I wish you as a personal friend of mine would tell him you have reason to believe he is mistaken. The truth is, I would like to go very much. Still, circumstances may happen which may prevent my being a candidate.

If there are any who be my friends in such an enterprise, what I now want is that they shall not throw me away just yet. Yours as ever

A. Lincoln

LETTER TO WILLIAM H. HERNDON

Washington, July 11—1848.

Dear William:

Yours of the 3rd is this moment received; and I hardly need say, it gives unalloyed pleasure. I now almost regret writing the serious, long faced letter, I wrote yesterday; but let the past as nothing be. Go it while you're young! I write this in the confusion of the H. R, and with several other things to attend to. I will send you about eight different speeches this evening; and as to kissing a pretty girl, I know one very pretty one, but I guess she won't let me kiss her.

Yours forever,
A Lincoln

NOTES FOR A LAW LECTURE

[*1st July 1850?*]

I am not an accomplished lawyer. I find quite as much material for a lecture in those points wherein I have failed, as in those wherein I have been moderately successful. The leading rule for the lawyer, as for the man of every other calling, is diligence. Leave nothing for to-morrow which can be done to-day. Never let your correspondence fall behind. Whatever piece of business you have in hand, before stopping, do all the labour pertaining to it which can then be done. When you bring a common-law suit, if you have the facts for doing so, write the declaration at once. If a law point be involved, examine the books and note the authority you rely on upon the declaration itself, where you are sure to find it when wanted. The same of defences and pleas. In business not likely to be litigated—ordinary collection cases, foreclosures, partitions, and the like—make all examinations of titles and note them, and even draft orders and decrees in advance. This course has a triple advantage; it avoids omissions and neglect, saves your labour when once done, performs the labour out of court when you have leisure, rather than in court when you have not. Extemporaneous speaking should be practised and cultivated. It is the lawyer's avenue to the public. However able and faithful he may be in other respects, people are slow to bring him business if he cannot make a speech. And yet there is not a more fatal error to young lawyers than relying too much on speech-making. If any-one, upon his rare powers of speaking, shall claim an exemption from the drudgery of the law, his case is a failure in advance.

Discourage litigation. Persuade your neighbours to compromise whenever you can. Point out to them how the nominal winner is often a real loser—in fees, expenses, and waste of time. As a peacemaker the lawyer has a superior opportunity of being a good man. There will still be business enough.

Never stir up litigation. A worse man can scarcely be found than one who does this. Who can be more nearly a fiend than he who habitually overhauls the register of deeds in search of defects in titles, whereon to stir up strife, and put money in his pocket? A moral tone ought to be infused into the profession which should drive such men out of it.

The matter of fees is important, far beyond the mere question of bread and butter involved. Properly attended to, fuller justice is done to both lawyer and client. An exorbitant fee should never be claimed. As a general rule never take your whole fee in advance, nor any more than a small retainer. When fully paid beforehand, you are more than a common mortal if you can feel the same interest in the case, as if something was still in prospect for you, as well as for your client. And when you lack interest in the case the job will very likely lack skill and diligence in the performance. Settle the amount of fee and take a note in advance. Then you will feel that you are working for something, and you are sure to do your work faithfully and well. Never sell a fee note—at least not before the consideration service is performed. It leads to negligence and dishonesty—negligence by losing interest in the case, and dishonesty in refusing to refund when you have allowed the consideration to fail.

There is a vague popular belief that lawyers are necessarily dishonest. I say vague, because when we consider to what extent confidence and honours are reposed in and conferred upon lawyers by the people, it appears improbable that their impression of dishonesty is very distinct and vivid. Yet the impression is common, almost universal. Let no young man choosing the law for a calling for a moment yield to the popular belief—resolve to be honest at all events; and if in your own judgment you cannot be an honest lawyer, resolve to be honest without being a lawyer. Choose some other occupation rather than one in

26

the choosing of which you do, in advance, consent to be a knave.

MEMORANDUM ON THE PRESIDENT'S DUTY IF NOT RE-ELECTED

23rd August 1864.

This morning, as for some days past, it seems exceedingly probable that this administration will not be re-elected. Then it will be my duty to so co-operate with the President-elect, as to save the Union between the election and the inauguration; as he will have secured his election on such ground that he cannot possibly save it afterwards.

After Lincoln's re-election in 1864 he noticed Stanton's joy that two of his opponents had lost. Lincoln told him: "You have more of that feeling of personal resentment than I. Perhaps I may have too little of it but I never thought it paid. A man has not time to spend half his life in quarrels."

III

Letters to
His Stepbrother
(JOHN D. JOHNSTON)

Dear Johnston:

Your request for eighty dollars I do not think it best to comply with now. At the various times when I have helped you a little, you have said to me, "We can get along very well now" but in a very short time I find you in the same difficulty again. Now this can only happen by some defect in your *conduct*. What that defect is, I think I know. You are not *lazy,* and still you *are* an *idler.* I doubt whether since I saw you, you have done a good whole day's work, in any one day. You do not very much dislike to work; and still you do not work much, merely because it does not seem to you that you could get much for it. This habit of uselessly wasting time, is the whole difficulty; and it is vastly important to you, and still more so to your children that you should break this habit. It is more important to them, because they have longer to live, and can keep out of an idle habit before they are in it, easier than they can get out after they are in.

You are now in need of some [ready?] money; and what I propose is, that you shall go to work, "tooth and nails" for somebody who will give you money for it. Let father and your boys take charge of things at home—prepare for a crop, and make the crop; and you go to work for the best money wages, or in discharge of any debt you owe, that you can get. And to secure you a fair reward for your labor, I now promise you that for every dollar you will, between this and the first of next May, get for your own labor, either in money, or on your own indebtedness, I will then give you one other dollar. By this, if you hire yourself at ten dolla[rs] a month, from me you will get ten more, making twenty dollars a month for your work. In this, I do not mean you shall go off to St. Louis, or the lead mines, or the gold mines in Calif[ornia,]

31

but I [mean for you to go at it for the best wages you] can get close to home in Coles county. Now if you will do this, you will be soon out of debt, and what is better, you will have a habit that will keep you from getting in debt again. But if I should now clear you out, next year you would be just as deep in as ever. You say you would almost give your place in Heaven for $70 or $80. Then you value your place in Heaven very cheapl[y] for I am sure you can with the offer I make you get the seventy or eighty dollars for four or five months work. You say if I furnish you the money you will deed me the land, and, if you don't pay the money back, you will deliver possession. Nonsense! If you can't now live *with* the land, how will you then live without it? You have always been [kind] to me, and I do not now mean to be unkind to you. On the contrary, if you will but follow my advice, you will find it worth more than eight times eighty dollars to you.

Affectionately
Your brother
A. Lincoln

Springfield, 12th January 1851.

Dear Brother: On the day before yesterday I received a letter from Harriett, written at Greenup. She says she has just returned from your house; and that Father is very low and will hardly recover. She also says you have written me two letters; and that, although you do not expect me to come now, you wonder that I do not write. I received both your letters, and although I have not answered them, it is not because I have forgotten them or been uninterested about them—but because it appeared to me I could write nothing which could do any good. You already know I desire that neither Father or Mother shall be in

32

want of any comfort either in health or sickness while they live and I feel sure you have not failed to use my name, if necessary, to procure a doctor, or anything else for Father in his present sickness. My business is such that I could hardly leave home now, if it were not, as it is, that my own wife is sick abed. (It is a case of baby-sickness, and I suppose is not dangerous.) I sincerely hope Father may yet recover his health; but at all events tell him to remember to call upon, and confide in, our great, and good, and merciful Maker, who will not turn away from him in any extremity. He notes the fall of a sparrow, and numbers the hairs of our heads; and He will not forget the dying man, who puts his trust in Him. Say to him that if we could meet now, it is doubtful whether it would not be more painful than pleasant; but that if it be his lot to go now, he will soon have a joyous meeting with many loved ones gone before; and where the rest of us, through the help of God, hope ere long to join them.

Write me again when you receive this. Affectionately
A. Lincoln

Shelbyville, November 4, 1851.

Dear Brother:

When I came into Charleston day before yesterday, I learned that you are anxious to sell the land where you live and move to Missouri. I have been thinking of this ever since, and cannot but think such a notion is utterly foolish. What can you do in Missouri better than here? Is the land any richer? Can you there, any more than here, raise corn and wheat and oats without work? Will anybody there, any more than here, do your work for you? If you intend to go to work, there is no better place than right where you are; if you do not intend to go to work, you cannot get along anywhere. Squirming and crawling about from place to place can do no good. You have raised no crop this year; and what you really want is to sell the land, get the money, and spend it. Part with the land you have, and, my life upon it, you will never after own a spot big enough to bury you in. Half you will get for the land you will spend in moving to Missouri, and the other half you will eat, drink, and wear out, and no foot of land will be bought. Now, I feel it my duty to have no hand in such a piece of foolery. I feel that it is so even on your own account, and particularly on mother's account. The eastern forty acres I intend to keep for mother while she lives; if you will not cultivate it, it will rent for enough to support her—at least, it will rent for something. Her dower in the other two forties she can let you have, and no thanks to me. Now, do not misunderstand this letter; I do not write it in any unkindness. I write it in order, if possible, to get you to face the truth, which truth is, you are destitute because you have idled away all your time. Your thousand pretenses for not getting along better are all nonsense; they deceive nobody but yourself. Go to work is the only cure for your case.

A word to mother. Chapman tells me he wants you to go and live with him. If I were you I would try it awhile. If you get tired of it (as I think you will not), you can return to your own home. Chapman feels very kindly to you, and I have no doubt he will make your situation very pleasant.

Sincerely your son,
A. Lincoln

Springfield, Novr. 25, 1851.

Dear Brother

Your letter of the 22nd. is just received. Your proposal about selling the East forty acres of land is all that I want or could claim for *myself*; but I am not satisfied with it on *Mother's* account. I want her to have her living, and I feel that it is my duty, to some extent, to see that she is not wronged. She had a right of Dower (that is, the use of one third for life) in the other two forties; but, it seems, she has already let you take that, hook and line. She now has the use of the whole of the East forty, as long as she lives; and if it be sold, of course, she is entitled to the interest on *all* the money it brings, as long as she lives; but you propose to sell it for three hundred dollars, take one hundred away with you, and leave her two hundred, at 8 per cent, making her the *enormous* sum of 16 dollars a year. Now, if you are satisfied with treating her in that way, I am not. It is true, that you are to have that forty for two hundred dollars, *at* Mother's death; but you are not to have it *before*. I am confident that land can be made to produce for Mother, at least $30 a year, and I can not, to oblige any living person, consent that she shall be put on an allowance of sixteen dollars a year.

Yours &c
A. Lincoln

IV

Letters to Ladies

TO MARY TODD LINCOLN

Washington, June 12. 1848—·

My dear wife:

On my return from Philadelphia, yesterday, where, in my anxiety I had been led to attend the whig convention, I found your last letter. I was so tired and sleepy, having ridden all night, that I could not answer it till to-day; and now I have to do so in the H. R. The leading matter in your letter, is your wish to return to the side of the mountains. Will you be a *good girl* in all things, if I consent? Then come along, and that as *soon* as possible. Having got the idea in my head, I shall be impatient till I see you. You will not have money enough to bring you; but I presume your uncle will supply you, and I will refund him here. By the way you do not mention whether you have received the fifty dollars I sent you. I do not much fear but that you got it; because the want of it would have induced you [to?] say something in relation to it. If your uncle is already at Lexington, you might induce him to start on earlier than the first of July; he could stay in Kentucky longer on his return, and so make up for lost time. Since I began this letter, the H. R. has passed a resolution for adjourning on the 17th. July, which probably will pass the Senate. I hope this letter will not be disagreeable to you; which, together with the circumstances under which I write, I hope will excuse me from not writing a longer one. Come on just as soon as you can. I want to see you, and our dear—*dear* boys very much. Every body here wants to see our dear Bobby.

Affectionately
A Lincoln

TO MARY TODD LINCOLN

Washington, July 2. 1848

My dear wife:

Your letter of last sunday came last night. On that day (sunday) I wrote the principal part of a letter to you, but did not finish it, or send it till tuesday, when I had provided a draft for $100 which I sent in it. It is now probable that on that day (tuesday) you started to Shelbyville; so that when the money reaches Lexington, you will not be there. Before leaving, did you make any provision about letters that might come to Lexington for you? Write me whether you got the draft, if you shall not have already done so, when this reaches you. Give my kindest regards to your uncle John, and all the family. Thinking of them reminds me that I saw your acquaintance, Newton, of Arkansas, at the Philadelphia Convention. We had but a single interview, and that was so brief, and in so great a multitude of strange faces, that I am quite sure I should not recognize him, if I were to meet him again. He was a sort of Trinity, three in one, having the right, in his own person, to cast the three votes of Arkansas. Two or three days ago I sent your uncle John, and a few of our other friends each a copy of the speech I mentioned in my last letter; but I did not send any to you, thinking you would be on the road here, before it would reach you. I send you one now. Last wednesday, P. H. Hood & Co, dunned me for a little bill of $5.38 cents, and Walter Harper & Co, another for $8.50 cents, for goods which they say you bought. I hesitated to pay them, because my recollection is that you told me when you went away, there was nothing left unpaid. Mention in your next letter whether they are right. Mrs. Richardson is still here; and what is more, has a baby—so Richardson says, and he ought to know. I believe Mary Hewett has left here and gone to Boston. I met her on the street about fifteen or twenty days ago, and she told me she was going soon. I have seen nothing of her since. The music in the Capitol grounds on saturdays, or, rather, the interest in it, is dwindling down to nothing. Yesterday evening the attendance was rather thin. Our two girls, whom you remember seeing first at Carusis, at the exhibition of the Ethiopian Serenaders, and whose peculiarities were the wearing of black fur bonnets, and never being seen in close company with other ladies, were at the music yesterday. One of them was attended by their brother, and the other had a member of Congress in tow. He went home with her; and if I were to guess, I would say, he went away a somewhat altered man—most likely in his pockets, and in some other particular. The fellow looked conscious of guilt, although I believe he was unconscious that every body around knew who it was that had caught him.

I have had no letter from home, since I wrote you before, except short business letters, which have no interest for you.

By the way, you do not intend to do without a girl, because the one you had has left you? Get another as soon as you can to take charge of the dear codgers. Father expected to see you all sooner; but let it pass; stay as long as you please, and come when you please. Kiss and love the dear rascals.

Affectionately
A. Lincoln

WRITTEN BY LINCOLN IN THE
AUTOGRAPH ALBUM OF
MARY DELAHAY
December 7, 1859

Dear Mary

With pleasure I write my name in your Album. Ere long some younger man will be more happy to confer *his* name upon *you*. Don't allow it, Mary, until fully assured that he is worthy of the happiness. Dec. 7—1859

Your friend
A. Lincoln

TO MRS. M. J. GREEN

Springfield, Ills. Sep. 22. 1860

Mrs. M. J. Green
My Dear Madam.

Your kind congratulatory letter, of August, was received in due course—and should have been answered sooner. The truth is I have never corresponded much with ladies; and hence I postpone writing letters to them, as a business which I do not understand. I can only say now I thank you for the good opinion you express of me, fearing, at the same time, I may not be able to maintain it through life.

Yours very truly
A. Lincoln.

TO MISS GRACE BEDELL

Private
Springfield, Ills. Oct. 19. 1860

Miss. Grace Bedell
My dear little Miss.

Your very agreeable letter of the 15th. is received.

I regret the necessity of saying I have no daughters. I have three sons—one seventeen, one nine, and one seven, years of age. They, with their mother, constitute my whole family.

As to the whiskers, having never worn any, do you not think people would call it a piece of silly affection if I were to begin it now—?

Your very sincere well-wisher

A. Lincoln.

TO MISS FANNY McCULLOUGH

Executive Mansion,
Washington, December 23., 1862.

Dear Fanny

It is with deep grief that I learn of the death of your kind and brave Father; and, especially, that it is affecting your young heart beyond what is common in such cases. In this sad world of ours, sorrow comes to all; and, to the young, it comes with bitterest agony, because it takes them unawares. The older have learned to ever expect it. I am anxious to afford some alleviation of your present distress. Perfect relief is not possible, except with time. You can not now realize that you will ever feel better. Is not this so? And yet it is a mistake. You are sure to be happy again. To know this, which is certainly true, will make you some less miserable now. I have had experience enough to know what I say; and you need only to believe it, to feel better at once. The memory of your dear Father, instead of an agony, will yet be a sad sweet feeling in

your heart, of a purer, and holier sort than you have
known before.

Please present my kind regards to your afflicted Mother.
Miss. Fanny McCullough.

Your sincere friend,
A. Lincoln.

TO MARY TODD LINCOLN

Executive Mansion,
Washington, August 8, 1863.

My dear Wife:

All as well as usual, and no particular trouble anyway.
I put the money into the Treasury at five per cent., with
the privilege of withdrawing it any time upon thirty days'
notice. I suppose you are glad to learn this. Tell dear Tad
poor "Nanny Goat" is lost, and Mrs. Cuthbert and I are
in distress about it. The day you left, Nanny was found
resting herself and chewing her little cud on the middle
of Tad's bed; but now she's gone! The gardener kept com-
plaining that she destroyed the flowers, till it was con-
cluded to bring her down to the White House. This was
done, and the second day she had disappeared and has
not been heard of since. This is the last we know of poor
"Nanny."

The weather continues dry and excessively warm here.
Nothing very important occurring. The election in Kentucky has gone very strongly right. Old Mr. Wickliffe got
ugly, as you know: ran for governor, and is terribly beaten.
Upon Mr. Crittenden's death, Brutus Clay, Cassius's
brother, was put on the track for Congress, and is largely
elected. Mr. Menzies, who, as we thought, behaved very
badly last session of Congress, is largely beaten in the

district opposite Cincinnati, by Green Clay Smith, Cassius Clay's nephew. But enough.

Affectionately,
A. Lincoln.

TO MRS. ELIZA P. GURNEY

Executive Mansion,
Washington, September 4., 1864.

Eliza P. Gurney.
My esteemed friend.

I have not forgotten—probably never shall forget—the very impressive occasion when yourself and friends visited me on a Sabbath forenoon two years ago. Nor has your kind letter, written nearly a year later, ever been forgotten. In all, it has been your purpose to strengthen my reliance on God. I am much indebted to the good Christian people of the country for their constant prayers and consolations; and to no one of them, more than to yourself. The purposes of the Almighty are perfect, and must prevail, though we erring mortals may fail to accurately perceive them in advance. We hoped for a happy termination of this terrible war long before this; but God knows best, and has ruled otherwise. We shall yet acknowledge His wisdom and our own error therein. Meanwhile we must work earnestly in the best light He gives us, trusting that so working still conduces to the great ends He ordains. Surely He intends some great good to follow this mighty convulsion, which no mortal could make, and no mortal could stay.

Your people—the Friends—have had, and are having, a very great trial. On principle, and faith, opposed to both war and oppression, they can only practically oppose oppression by war. In this hard dilemma, some have chosen one horn, and some the other. For those appealing to me on conscientious grounds, I have done, and shall do, the best I could and can, in my own conscience, under my oath to the law. That you believe this I doubt not; and believing it, I shall still receive, for our country and myself, your earnest prayers to our Father in heaven.

Your sincere friend
A. Lincoln.

TO MRS. BIXBY

Executive Mansion,
Washington, Nov. 21, 1864.

Dear Madam,—

I have been shown in the files of the war Department a statement of the Adjutant General of Massachusetts, that you are the mother of five sons who have died gloriously on the field of battle.

I feel how weak and fruitless must be any word of mine which should attempt to beguile you from the grief of a loss so overwhelming. But I cannot refrain from tendering to you the consolation that may be found in the thanks of the Republic they died to save.

I pray that our Heavenly Father may assuage the anguish of your bereavement, and leave you only the cherished memory of the loved and lost, and the solemn pride that must be yours, to have laid so costly a sacrifice upon the altar of Freedom.

Yours, very sincerely and respectfully,
A. Lincoln

Mrs. Bixby.

V

Letters to Generals

t

TO GENERAL G. B. McCLELLAN,
COMMANDING THE
ARMY OF THE POTOMAC

3rd February 1862.

My Dear Sir: You and I have distinct, and different plans for a movement of the Army of the Potomac—yours to be down the Chesapeake, up the Rappahannock to Urbana, and across land to the terminus of the railroad on the York River—mine to move directly to a point on the railroad south-west of Manassas.

If you will give me satisfactory answers to the following questions, I shall gladly yield my plan to yours.

1st. Does not your plan involve a greatly larger expenditure of *time,* and *money* than mine?

2nd. Wherein is a victory *more certain* by your plan than mine?

3rd. Wherein is a victory *more valuable* by your plan than mine?

4th. In fact, would it not be *less* valuable, in this, that it would break no great line of the enemy's communications, while mine would?

5th. In case of disaster, would not a safe retreat be more difficult by your plan than by mine?   Yours truly

A. Lincoln

[MEMORANDUM ACCOMPANYING LETTER]

1. Suppose the enemy should attack us in force *before* we reach the Ocoquan, what? In view of the possibility of this, might it not be safest to have our entire force to move together from above the Ocoquan?

2. Suppose the enemy, in force, shall dispute the crossing of the Ocoquan, what? In view of this, might it not be

safest for us to cross the Ocoquan at Colchester rather than at the village of Ocoquan? This would cost the enemy two miles more of travel to meet us, but would, on the contrary, leave us two miles further from our ultimate destination.

3. Suppose we reach Maple valley without an attack, will we not be attacked there, in force, by the enemy marching by the several roads from Manassas? and if so, what?

TELEGRAM TO GENERAL
G. B. McCLELLAN

Washington City, D. C. July 5. 1862.

Major Genl. McClellan

A thousand thanks for the relief your two despatches of 12 & 1 P.M. yesterday give me. Be assured the heroism and skill of yourself, officers, and men, are, and forever will be appreciated. If you can hold your present position, we shall *"hive"* the enemy yet.

A. Lincoln

TO GENERAL G. B. McCLELLAN

Executive Mansion,
Washington, July 13 1862.

Major General McClellan
My dear Sir—

I am told that over 160-000 men have gone into your Army on the Peninsula. When I was with you the other day we made out 86,500 remaining, leaving 73,500 to be accounted for. I believe 23,500 will cover all the killed, wounded and missing in all your battles and skirmishes, leaving 50-000 who have left otherwise. Not more than 5000 of these have died, leaving 45-000 of your Army still alive, and not with it. I believe half, or two thirds of them are fit for duty to-day. Have you any more perfect knowledge of this than I have? If I am right, and you had these men with you, you could go into Richmond in the next three days. How can they be got to you? and how can they be prevented from getting away in such numbers for the future?

A. Lincoln

TELEGRAM TO GENERAL
G. B. McCLELLAN

Washington, D. C., Sep. 15, 2:45 1862.

Major General McClellan.
Your despatches of to-day received. God bless you, and all with you. Destroy the rebel army, if possible.

A. Lincoln

TELEGRAM TO GENERAL
G. B. McCLELLAN

Washington City, D. C. Oct. 24. 1862

Majr. Genl. McClellan
I have just read your despatch about sore tongued and fatigued horses.
Will you pardon me for asking what the horses of your army have done since the battle of Antietam that fatigue anything?

A. Lincoln

TELEGRAM TO GENERAL
G. B. McCLELLAN

Executive Mansion,
Washington, Oct. 27, 1862

Majr. Gen. McClellan.

Yours of yesterday received. Most certainly I intend
no injustice to any; and if I have done any, I deeply regret
it. To be told after more than five weeks total inaction of
the Army, and during which period we had sent to that
Army every fresh horse we possibly could, amounting in
the whole to 7918 that the cavalry horses were too much
fatigued to move, presented a very cheerless, almost hope-
less, prospect for the future; and it may have forced something of impatience into my despatches. If not recruited,
and rested then, when could they ever be? I suppose the
river is rising, and I am glad to believe you are crossing.

A. Lincoln

TO GENERAL ULYSSES S. GRANT, WHO
HAD RECENTLY TAKEN VICKSBURG

13th July 1863.

My dear General: I do not remember that you and I
ever met personally. I write this now as a grateful acknowledgment for the almost inestimable service you have
done the country. I wish to say a word further. When
you first reached the vicinity of Vicksburg, I thought you
should do what you finally did—march the troops across
the neck, run the batteries with the transports, and thus
go below; and I never had any faith, except a general hope
that you knew better than I, that the Yazoo Pass expedi-
tion, and the like, could succeed. When you got below

and took Port Gibson, Grand Gulf, and vicinity, I thought you should go down the river and join Gen. Banks; and when you turned northward east of the Big Black, I feared it was a mistake. I now wish to make the personal acknowledgment that you were right, and I was wrong. Yours very truly

A. Lincoln

TELEGRAM TO GENERAL G. G. MEADE

Washington, D. C., Oct. 8. 1863

Major General Meade
Army of Potomac

I am appealed to in behalf of August Blittersdorf, at Mitchells Station, Va. to be shot to-morrow, as a deserter. I am unwilling for any boy under eighteen to be shot; and his father affirms that he is yet under sixteen. Please answer. His Regt. or Co. not given me.

A. Lincoln

TO GENERAL ULYSSES S. GRANT

Executive Mansion Washington,

Lieutenant General Grant.   *April 30, 1864*

Not expecting to see you again before the Spring campaign opens, I wish to express, in this way, my entire satisfaction with what you have done up to this time, so far as I understand it. The particulars of your plans I neither know, or seek to know. You are vigilant and self-reliant; and, pleased with this, I wish not to obtrude any constraints or restraints upon you. While I am very anxious that any great disaster, or the capture of our men in great numbers, shall be avoided, I know these points are less likely to escape your attention than they would be mine. If there is anything wanting which is within my power to give, do not fail to let me know it.

And now with a brave Army, and a just cause, may God sustain you.   Yours very truly

A. Lincoln

TELEGRAM TO GENERAL ULYSSES S. GRANT, BESIEGING RICHMOND

17th August 1864.

I have seen your dispatch expressing your unwillingness to break your hold where you are.   Neither am I willing. Hold on with a bulldog grip, and chew and choke, as much as possible.

TELEGRAM TO GENERAL GRANT
April, 1865

Gen. Sheridan says "If the thing is pressed I think that Lee will surrender." Let the thing be pressed.

VI

Wit and Wisdom

A funny story, if it has the element of genuine wit, has the same effect on me that I suppose a good square drink of whiskey has on an old toper; it puts new life into me.

In times like the present, men should utter nothing for which they would not willingly be responsible through time and in eternity.

LETTER TO MAJOR G. D. RAMSAY

Executive Mansion
Oct. 17, 1861

Majr. Ramsay
My dear Sir
The lady—bearer of this—says she has two sons who want work. Set them at it, if possible. Wanting to work is so rare a merit, that it should be encouraged

Yours truly
A. Lincoln

Fellow-citizens, we cannot escape history.

The will of God prevails. In great contests each party claims to act in accordance with the will of God. Both may be, and one must be, wrong. God cannot be for and against the same thing at the same time. In the present civil war it is quite possible that God's purpose is something different from the purpose of either party; and yet the human instrumentalities, working just as they do, are of the best adaptation to effect his purpose. I am almost ready to say that this is probably true; that God wills this contest, and wills that it shall not end yet. By his mere great power on the minds of the now contestants, he could have either saved or destroyed the Union without a human contest. Yet the contest began. And, having begun, he could give the final victory to either side any day. Yet the contest proceeds.

If we could first know where we are, and whither we are tending, we could better judge what to do, and how to do it.

The strongest bond of human sympathy, outside of the family relation, should be one uniting all working people, of all nations, and tongues, and kindreds. Nor should this lead to a war upon property, or the owners of property. Property is the fruit of labor—property is desirable—is a positive good in the world. That some should be rich, shows that others may become rich, and hence is just encouragement to industry and enterprise. Let not him who is houseless pull down the house of another; but let him labor diligently and build one for himself, thus by example assuring that his own shall be safe from violence when built.

Whenever I hear anyone, arguing for slavery I feel a strong impulse to see it tried on him personally.

LETTER TO E. M. STANTON, SECRETARY OF WAR

Executive Mansion,
Washington, Nov. 11, 1863.

Hon. Secretary of War.
My dear Sir:
    I personally wish Jacob R. Freese, of New-Jersey, to be

appointed a Colonel for a colored regiment—and this regardless of whether he can tell the exact shade of Julius Caesars hair.

Yours truly
A. Lincoln

Let us have faith that right makes might, and in that faith, let us, to the end, dare to do our duty as we understand it.

True Democracy makes no inquiry about the color of the skin, or place of nativity, or any other similar circumstances of condition. I regard, therefore, the exclusion of the colored people as a body from the elective franchise as incompatible with true Democratic principles.

Labor is prior to, and independent of, capital. Capital is only the fruit of labor, and could never have existed if labor had not first existed. Labor is the superior of capital, and deserves much the higher consideration. Capital has its rights, which are as worthy of protection as any other rights. Nor is it denied that there is, and probably always will be, a relation between labor and capital producing mutual benefts.

As I would not be a *slave,* so I would not be a *master.* This expresses my idea of democracy. Whatever differs from this, to the extent of the difference, is not democracy.

The sympathies of this country and the benefits of its position should be exerted in favor of the people of every nation struggling to be free.

My declarations upon this subject of Negro slavery may be misrepresented, but cannot be misunderstood. I have said that I do not understand the Declaration to mean that all men were created equal in all respects. They are not our equal in colour; but I suppose that it does mean to declare that all men are equal in some respects; they are equal in their right to "life, liberty, and the pursuit of happiness." Certainly the Negro is not our equal in colour—perhaps not in many other respects; still, in the right to put into his mouth the bread that his own hands have earned, he is the equal of every other man, white or black. In pointing out that more has been given you, you cannot be justified in taking away the little which has been given him. All I ask for the Negro is that if you do not like him, let him alone. If God gave him but little, that little let him enjoy.

I am glad to see that a system of labor prevails in New England under which laborers can strike when they want to, where they are not obliged to work under all circumstances, and are not tied down and obliged to labor whether you pay them or not!

I know the trials and woes of working men, and I have always felt for them. I know that in almost every case of strikes, the men have just cause for complaint.

This is a world of compensation; and he who would *be* no slave, must consent to *have* no slave. Those who deny freedom to others, deserve it not for themselves; and, under a just God, can not long retain it.

In the early days of our race the Almighty said to the first of our race, "In the sweat of thy face shalt thou eat bread"; and since then, if we except the light and the air of heaven, no good thing has been or can be enjoyed by us without having first cost labor. And inasmuch as most good things are produced by labor, it follows that all such things of right belong to those whose labor has produced them. But it has so happened, in all ages of the world, that some have labored, and others have without labor enjoyed a large proportion of the fruits. This is wrong, and should not continue. To secure to each laborer the whole product of his labor, or as nearly as possible, is a worthy object of any good government.

I am not a Know-Nothing. That is certain. How could I be? How can any one who abhors the oppression of negroes, be in favor of degrading classes of white people? Our progress in degeneracy appears to me to be pretty rapid. As a nation, we began by declaring that *"all men are created equal."* We now practically read it "all men are created equal, *except negroes"* When the Know-Nothings get control, it will read "all men are created equal, except negroes, *and foreigners, and Catholics."* When it comes to this I should prefer emigrating to some country where they make no pretence of loving liberty—to Russia, for instance, where despotism can be taken pure, and without the base alloy of hypocracy [*sic*].

This country, with its institutions, belongs to the people who inhabit it. Whenever they shall grow weary of the existing government, they can exercise their constitutional right of amending it, or their revolutionary right to dismember or overthrow it.

While I have often said that all men ought to be free, yet I would allow those colored persons to be slaves who want to be; and next to them those white persons who argue in favor of making other people slaves. I am in favor of giving an opportunity to such white men to try it on for themselves.

I should like to know if taking this old Declaration of Independence, which declares that all men are equal upon principle and making exceptions to it where will it stop. If one man says it does not mean a Negro, why not another say it does not mean some other man?

As a *good* thing, slavery is strikingly peculiar in this, that it is the only good thing which no man ever seeks the good of, for himself.

Lincoln described a certain lawyer in these words: "He can compress the most words into the smallest ideas of any man I ever saw."

In 1864 Francis Bicknell Carpenter painted a portrait of Lincoln with his cabinet. At that time Salmon P. Chase was writing to people all over the country about Lincoln's weakness and vacillation and trying his best to get himself nominated for the next term of the Presidency in Lincoln's place, while the unhappiness of other cabinet members with Lincoln was marked. Carpenter observed that one day Lincoln turned to a friend in the Senate and said with a sly twinkle in his eye: "Mrs. Lincoln calls Mr. Carpenter's group the happy family."

The bloodshed of the Civil War gave the President great anguish. He once said to Congressman Daniel Voorhees, "Voorhees, don't it seem strange to you that I who could never so much as cut off the head of a chicken, should be elected, or selected, into the midst of all this blood?"

General Grant was constantly criticized for his alleged recklessness and his fondness for whiskey. When one visitor complained to Lincoln about the latter failing, the President, who rarely drank, said: "Find out what brand he drinks and send some to my other generals."

A. K. McClure spent two hours with Lincoln one night, voicing the opinion of many of Lincoln's friends that the President would be ruined if he retained Grant. After citing every argument he could think of, McClure paused. After a long silence Lincoln said, "I can't spare this man; *he fights.*"

During the Civil War a delegation visited Lincoln demanding a position for General John C. Fremont. Lincoln said he would give Fremont a position if he could, but he could not without replacing some other general. He added that he was reminded of a story about the old man who kept advising his son to take a wife. The boy asked, "Whose wife shall I take?"

At the funeral of a pompous officer, Lincoln said: "If the general had known he'd get a funeral like this, he'd have died far sooner."

While Grant's campaign moved forward, one man told Lincoln that he would surely be re-elected President unless Grant captured Richmond, in which case the Democrats would nominate Grant. Lincoln answered: "Well, I feel very much like the man who said he didn't want to die particularly, but if he had got to die that was precisely the disease he would like to die of."

In May of 1864 General John C. Fremont, who had been the Republican candidate for President in 1856, organized a radical new political party called Radical Democracy. Fremont, of course, was nominated. The next day a friend told Lincoln about the convention of the new party, commenting that only 400 people had been present. President Lincoln reached for the Bible on his desk and read these words: "And everyone that was in distress, and everyone that was in debt, and everyone that was discontented, gathered themselves unto him; and he became a captain over them; and there were with him about four hundred men."

Of a mendacious visitor Lincoln said, "He reminds me of an old fisherman I used to know who got such a reputation for stretching the truth that he bought a pair of scales and insisted on weighing every fish in the presence of witnesses. One day a baby was born next door and the doctor borrowed the fisherman's scales. The baby weighed forty-seven pounds."